Original title:
In the Shadow of Palms

Copyright © 2025 Creative Arts Management OÜ
All rights reserved.

Author: Adrian Caldwell
ISBN HARDBACK: 978-1-80581-489-4
ISBN PAPERBACK: 978-1-80581-016-2
ISBN EBOOK: 978-1-80581-489-4

The Hushed Whispers of Nature's Veil

Beneath the fronds, a squirrel danced,
With acorns clutched, he pranced and pranced.
His tiny paws, a blur to see,
As if he'd won a nut-filled spree.

The breeze would giggle, rustling leaves,
While nearby rabbits donned their cheves.
A butterfly, with wings so bright,
Chased a gopher; what a sight!

A lizard lounged on sunlit stone,
Claiming his throne, though quite alone.
He winked at birds up on a wire,
Who sang of worms and their desire.

A chubby turtle, slow but wise,
Debated birds on soaring skies.
"Just take your time," he said with glee,
"Life's more fun when you stroll with me!"

And when the sun began to set,
The shadows laughed, no hint of regret.
In every rustle, chuckles flowed,
Nature's humor, a life bestowed.

Guardian of the Sunlit Glade

In a glade where sunlight plays,
A chicken danced in silly ways.
He strutted proud, with feathers bright,
Claiming the day, from morn to night.

The squirrels giggled from the trees,
While ants marched on, quite hard to please.
The rabbit rolled, a laugh-filled sight,
As shadows shrank with fading light.

Twilight Under the Feathered Leaves

A parrot perched on a swaying limb,
Singing songs that were quite dim.
His feathers fluffed, a bright display,
Mispronouncing words in a funny way.

The owls hooted, oh what a scene,
In a language that was rarely seen.
They swapped some tales, with a wink and laugh,
As the sun dipped low, on its final path.

Beneath the Hardwood Halo

Beneath the branches, a lizard grinned,
While mischief in his eyes did blend.
He told tall tales of daring do,
And how he charmed a wild kangaroo.

The toad joined in, with a croak and leap,
Claiming secrets the forest keeps.
In laughter's hold, they spun their lore,
Until the moon knocked on the door.

Lullabies of the Lush Haven

A raccoon strummed on a leafy lute,
With rhythm unmatched, oh what a hoot!
While fireflies danced, with lanterns bright,
The nighttime turned into pure delight.

The crickets chirped a lively beat,
As frogs joined in, with webbed feet.
Together they sang 'neath the starlit sky,
With giggles that made the universe sigh.

Reflections in a Shaded Haven

Underneath those leafy shades,
A party of squirrels plays charades.
The sunlight peeks, a shy old friend,
While ants march forth without an end.

Lizards bask like tiny kings,
Debating all the latest things.
A breeze comes by, with jokes to share,
The trees just giggle without a care.

Caress of the Tropical Breeze

A breeze winks through the vibrant green,
Tugging at my shirt, a playful scene.
It whispers tales of days gone by,
And twirls my hat up to the sky.

Coconuts roll like misfit toys,
Excited chirps from small, loud boys.
They chase the wind, with grins so wide,
While shadows dance, their glee can't hide.

The Woven Silence of Nature

The quiet hum of nature's call,
Where even silence seems to sprawl.
A frog croaks out a comic tune,
While crickets snap their own cartoons.

Hummingbirds zoom like comic sprites,
In search of nectar, quick delights.
With every flutter, laughter grows,
As nature plays—its quirks expose.

Glistening Whispers in the Wind

Whispers of laughter in the leaves,
As butterflies play hide and weave.
The flowers nod, without a fuss,
While bees agree, "It's time to buzz!"

Sunlight splashes, a golden jest,
While shadows play their silent quest.
In this bright realm, so full of cheer,
Even the bugs seem to persevere.

Dancing Light Through Emerald Canopy

Sunbeam giggles through the trees,
Tickling toes with playful breeze.
Laughter bounces, whispers blend,
As nature's dance begins to bend.

Creepy critters join the fun,
A squirrel twirls; a lizard runs.
Each leaf laughs at hues so bright,
A party hosted by pure light.

Echos of the Rustling Leaves

Leaves chat gossip in the air,
"Did you see that squirrel's flair?"
Ticklish winds spill out the tease,
While branches sway with giggling ease.

Whispers blend, a secret flow,
Frogs join in; they steal the show.
With every rustle comes a joke,
As nature laughs beneath the oak.

Beneath the Watchful Palms

Palms stand guard, all wise and tall,
   Coconut dreams await the fall.
A monkey swings from twig to bark,
   Yelling jokes that spark a lark.

Underneath their leafy reign,
Frisky ants march on a train.
No heavy mood by day or night,
Just cheeky fun and pure delight.

The Calm Before the Twilight

Daylight winks, then takes a break,
The frogs rehearse their evening cake.
As shadows play their nightly game,
The crickets chirp a tune, so lame.

Breezes whisper, 'Don't you dare,
Try to nap without a care.'
Twilight giggles, sets the stage,
For night's dance on a golden page.

Echoing Laughter Under the Sunlight

The sunbeams dance like silly fools,
As coconut fell, breaking the rules.
A parrot squawks in a funny way,
While we giggle the sunny day away.

A crab cartwheels, showing his style,
We laugh as he stumbles, all in a pile.
Sandcastles collapse, waves rolling near,
Life's just a joke, let's all cheer!

Reverberations of the Tropic Heart

The breeze chuckles, whispers a jest,
As flip-flops squeak, ain't this the best?
A mango slips, splat on my toes,
Everyone laughs, from head to nose.

A hammock swings, like laughter it lingers,
While I reach for fruit with sticky fingers.
The sun sets low with a wink and a grin,
Tomorrow's adventures are sure to begin!

Time Lost Among the Swaying Giants

Tall trees sway, like they're in a dance,
While I trip over roots, not a chance!
A breeze pulls my hat, off it goes,
Chasing it down, oh, how it flows!

Laughter echoes through the leafy maze,
As squirrels stare, caught in a daze.
Tickled by shadows, we stumble and roll,
Nature's humor feeds the soul!

Reflections Under the Leaves

Under the shade, we share silly tales,
While bugs dance around, outfitted in scales.
The sun peeks through, a curious spy,
We laugh at the clouds floating by.

A picnic unfolds, with ants in a rush,
Everyone's giggling, oh what a crush!
Checkered blanket, lemonade spills,
Laughter rings out, we bask in the thrills!

Enigma of the Verdant Shelter

Beneath the fronds so tall and wide,
A curious piglet tried to hide.
He wore a hat, quite dapper too,
But they found him stuck in a shoe!

Parrots squawked in a cheeky song,
While a monkey swung, quite strong.
With acorns raining from above,
Squirrel shook paws, just in love!

Diaphanous Shades of Solitude

A turtle danced with perfectly slow moves,
In a patch of light, he found his groove.
Chasing a shadow, he soared so high,
Until his friend said, 'You can't fly!"

Grasshoppers giggled, quite in the game,
As they hopscotched through their leafy fame.
A beetle dressed for a roaring show,
With buttons made of a pearly glow!

Life's Tapestry Woven in Green

A frog donned shades, as cool as can be,
Paddling through with fanciful glee.
He called out, 'Come join the fun,
We'll sip on dew when the day is done!'

Bumblebees buzzing, played hide and seek,
In blooms so bright, with colors unique.
But one got stuck in a flowered charm,
Yelling, 'Help! This plant means no harm!'

Twilight's Embrace in the Light

As dusk fell down, the fireflies danced,
A snail with a top hat pranced.
'Why wait for night?' the crickets sang,
'When in the woods, we can all just hang!'

The raccoons peeked from a leafy grin,
'Is that a party? Let's jump right in!'
With munchies made of sweet, sweet treats,
They laughed till dawn, in happy beats!

Enchanted Moments in the Quiet Grove

Amidst the green, a squirrel danced,
With acorns hatched, he took a chance.
He tripped and rolled, what a sight!
The trees just chuckled, oh what a night!

A frog in shades sat on a log,
Complaining loud, "Where's my fog?"
His croaks rang out, a cheerful tune,
While fireflies twinkled like stars at noon.

Murmurs of Secrets in the Breeze

Leaves whispered tales, they couldn't keep,
Of a raccoon who thought he could leap.
He missed the branch, oh what a fumble!
Landed in mud, and boy did he grumble!

A parrot squawked, "Look here, dear friend!"
As two rabbits argued, on gossip they'd spend.
Their fluffy ears perked, a scandal or two,
Every critter paused, they needed the view!

Where Green Skies Meet Canopy

A lizard strutted, flair to the max,
Wearing shades, laid back on the tracks.
He sunbathed bold, a smooth-talking champ,
While bees buzzed past, a hectic stamp!

An owl hooted jokes, oh what a wisecrack,
While beetles played cards, no skill they lack.
The trees swayed gently, joining the fun,
In this weird world, life's never done!

Gleams of Light Through the Green

Sunbeams flickered like a game of tag,
Chasing the shadows as they began to brag.
A turtle cheered, "Hey, keep it light!"
As shadows raced off, what a silly flight!

The ants held a meeting, but who would preside?
One stumbled in, wearing crumbs as his pride.
With laughter and crumbs, they all did agree,
Life in the leaves is the best way to be!

Echoes of Tropic Dreams

The monkey stole my hat, you see,
Now it's swinging on a tree.
I chase it round, a silly race,
That rascal grins, oh what a face!

A parrot squawks, a joke it tells,
It's better than my ringing bells.
The lizards dance to some old tune,
I think they party 'neath the moon.

The crabs walk sideways, quite a sight,
They scurry past, just shy of fright.
I throw them snacks, they wave goodbye,
While I, with laughter, ask them why.

As sunset hues begin to melt,
The mischief here is truly felt.
With every giggle and wild cheer,
These tropic dreams, I hold so dear.

Beneath the Tropical Veil

A coconut fell right on my head,
I sat and laughed, fell back instead!
The breeze comes by, it's quite a tease,
It whispers secrets through the trees.

A turtle munches on my shoe,
I swear he thinks it's buffet stew.
He nods and chews, "This looks just great,"
I'd join him, but I'm running late.

With fronds that wave like arms in glee,
The iguanas play tag with me.
They leap, they dive, in leaps so grand,
It's like a circus, oh, so planned!

The sun dips low, the fun won't cease,
With every giggle, there's release.
In twilight's laugh, we join the game,
In this wild place, we'll stake our claim.

A Soft Breeze in the Grove

There's a rustle that makes me smile,
It's just a squirrel with style!
He flips and flops, a furry show,
With acorn tricks he likes to throw.

The breeze thinks it's a game to play,
It tickles noses, leads astray.
We dance together, me and air,
A funny waltz without a care.

The flowers giggle, colors bright,
All bloom together, pure delight.
I ask a rose, "What's so amusing?"
It twirls and winks, no sign of bruising.

As stars appear, we twinkle too,
With laughter shared, the night feels new.
Beneath this sky, in joy we roam,
In every breath, we find our home.

Murmurs from the Palm Fronds

The palm trees whisper gossip loud,
About the tourists, quite a crowd.
With floppy hats and big sunblock,
They waddle by like a lost flock.

A flamingo winks, it struts its stuff,
With one leg up, it's really tough.
It critiques poses, quite the judge,
In this beach clique, it won't budge.

The breeze plays pranks, a feathery touch,
It flips my drink, I laugh so much.
Palm fronds sway, they join the tune,
While I serenade the silver moon.

In every wave and rambunctious cheer,
The tropical life draws us near.
With every chuckle ringing clear,
These silly moments bring pure cheer.

Shade of the Ancient Giants

Beneath the giant's leafy hat,
I spotted a lazy, sunbaked cat.
It eyed my sandwich, with a sly grin,
While plotting to sneak in for a win.

The breeze whispered jokes, with a slight tease,
I laughed so hard, dropped crumbs from my knees.
The palm leaves shook in a chuckling spree,
As the cat licked its paws, oh so carefree.

The Palm's Enigmatic Gaze

Those boughs above seem to know all,
Whispers of gossip from creatures small.
A squirrel debated with a crow,
On the best way to steal the show.

All the while, the palms maintain poise,
As their shadows dance, making odd noise.
Perhaps the trees giggle, when no one's near,
Transforming my picnic into a comedy sphere.

Tides of Time and Tranquility

Time drifts like a lazy old boat,
While I chase my sandwich, oh it won't float!
The waves of laughter crash on the sand,
As I trip over flip-flops, just as planned.

The palms stand firm, with a knowing stare,
Watching my tumble, their branches aware.
They sway and they wiggle, a comical show,
As I pick up my pride, and let out a 'whoa!'

Lullabies of the Leafy Dome

Beneath the canopy, a nap I took,
Dreaming of cookies from an old cookbook.
But the rustling leaves started to chime,
Singing sweet songs, not quite in time.

A parrot perched, with a voice so bold,
Coyly imitating, stories untold.
I giggled aloud, my dreams went away,
As the palms threw a party, in their own funny way.

Lush Secrets of the Tropics

A parrot jokes from a tree,
Its colors bright, a sight to see.
With cheeky caws it shouts, "Hey there!"
While monkeys swing without a care.

The iguana sunbathes with style,
Eyebrows raised, it wears a smile.
A coconut drops from above,
And sends all critters on the run!

Swaying palms whisper secrets near,
Lizards dance without a fear.
A tropical breeze carries a laugh,
As crabs join in for their own math.

With the sun setting in its glee,
No worries here, just jubilee.
A frog leaps in with perfect flair,
While all the world finds joy to share.

Echoes of the Green Oasis

Beneath the leaves, the critters plot,
A slug has dreams, though moves a lot.
His friends just laugh, they think it's fate,
To race the tortoise would be great!

A cactus grins in silence wide,
While cacti friends just roll and slide.
A chameleon shows off its hue,
With every shade, a laugh or two.

The breeze takes whispers from the grass,
As ants parade and strut with class.
A ruffled feather floats on by,
The troop stops short, lets out a sigh.

Our green oasis hides the fun,
With antics bright under the sun.
In laughter's arms, all creatures play,
To chase their worries far away.

Dance of Leaves at Dusk

When evening falls, the leaves begin,
To sway and twirl, a dance within.
A troupe of bugs joins in the show,
While fireflies flicker, putting on glow.

A squirrel drops acorns from high,
Winking at all, saying, "Oh my!"
The breeze teases branches with grace,
While shadows play in a shy embrace.

A lizard slips, a comic slip,
As all around erupt in giggleship.
The night brings out a lively tune,
Under the watchful, chuckling moon.

Each leaf a dancer, twirling swift,
Nature's laughter, the perfect gift.
A melody of fun unfolds,
In the dusky depths where joy enfolds.

Souls Adrift in the Breeze

On sandy shores, the crabs do prance,
They shuffle sideways, a funny dance.
With tiny top hats, they take the lead,
As laughter bubbles up like a seed.

The gulls squawk outrageous tales,
While riding winds and setting sails.
They tease the waves with their flapping feet,
As they paint the sky with jokes so neat.

Drifting leaves, they twirl and spin,
In their grand game, they all join in.
A leaf takes flight on a whim so bold,
While stories of the breeze are retold.

As the sun dips low, the giggles rise,
A symphony of nature's surprise.
With every gust, it's clear to see,
Souls drift light, wild, and silly, like spree.

Tranquil Murmurs of the Tropical Night

Beneath the stars, a gentle breeze,
Whispers of creatures, secrets tease.
A coconut falls with a startled thud,
While crickets chirp, in a quirky flood.

Lizards dance on the garden wall,
Wearing their suits, they're dressed for a ball.
With every rustle, a giggle breaks,
As the night plays tricks, and laughter wakes.

The moon is cheeky, peeking in,
Casting shadows on the palm's din.
A dance of light in a goofy spree,
While owls hoot sweetly in melody.

Jellyfishes down by the shore,
Partying hard, wanting more and more.
So join the fun, it's quite a sight,
In this whimsical, tropical night.

The Hidden Beauty of Swaying Giants

Tall silhouettes that sway and sway,
Winking at clouds, with roots at play.
Each leaf a hat, they tip and cheer,
Grooving around through the year.

A parrot squawks, a colorful sight,
Cackling loudly, it's quite a fright!
While monkeys swing with such finesse,
Cracking jokes, they're quite the mess.

Beneath the giants, laughter grows,
Tickling toes as the warm breeze blows.
With every sway, they jest and tease,
Offering shade with gentle ease.

No need for serious, not tonight,
Let's have some fun in the pale moonlight.
The giants grin, as if to say,
"Join us now, let's dance and play!"

Crescendo of Life in the Shade

Rustling leaves, a concert starts,
Each critter plays with joyful hearts.
The frogs croak deep, with bass in check,
While bugs join in, a lively trek.

A squirrel dives for a nutty treat,
Stumbling once, it lands on its feet.
The laughter bounces off the ground,
In the shade, joy is easily found.

Birds tweet the verses, sweet and high,
While shadows dance beneath the sky.
A symphony of oddities,
Playing notes of pure ecstasies.

Come join this merry serenade,
Let worries drift, like a passing shade.
In this fun-filled life, let's partake,
In this crescendo, let's make no mistake!

Essence of Roots and Fronds

The roots are plotting, deep below,
Whispering tales of long ago.
While fronds are swaying, catching rays,
In a sunlit waltz, through playful days.

A raccoon stumbles with a grin,
Searching for snacks, let the feast begin!
While beetles march in a funny line,
Making their way for a friend's fine dine.

The scent of blossoms fills the air,
While giggles float, without a care.
In the corners, mischief lingers,
As vines weave laughter with their fingers.

So come and join this lively space,
Where every nook is a happy place.
The roots and fronds keep spirits bright,
In this tangled mess of pure delight.

Breath of Life Among the Palms

Breeze tickles leaves, they start to dance,
A monkey swings by, lost in romance.
Sipping coconut water, oh what a scene,
Just me and my thoughts, living the dream.

The sun rises high, a golden delight,
I trip on a root, oh what a sight!
Laughter erupts from the critters nearby,
As I wipe off the sand, a seagull flies by.

Lost in the wonder, where wild things roam,
Each breeze whispers secrets, I call it home.
The palm leaves chuckle, as shadows play,
I wonder what they'd say if they had their way.

At dusk, when it cools, I'll settle right here,
Join in the chorus, every creature near.
With a wink from a lizard and an owl's soft hoot,
Life's a grand party, in nature's own suit.

Serenade of the Verdant Shadows

Under wide leaves, in a lively glade,
A bug's serenade, quite unafraid.
The parrots gossip, squawking with glee,
While I step on a squishy, wet pea.

A snail races past, oh what a feat!
We'll hold a debate on who's quicker on feet.
The palms lean in, like they're part of the jest,
As the sun starts to set, urging us west.

Sunbeams are dancing, like they're on a spree,
As I trip over roots that chuckle with me.
A shadowy specter, a shape on the ground,
I wave to my shadow, the friend that I've found.

With stars making plans to light up the night,
Those palms sing the tunes, and everything's right.
In this jolly haven, with laughter and cheer,
Nature's the maestro, the best volunteer.

Nestled Dreams Beneath the Leaves

Swaying like dancers, the leaves take their stage,
While I read a book about a wise old sage.
But the pages blow shut, with a gust of surprise,
A chipmunk jumps out with his mischievous eyes.

In this leafy retreat, there's a party tonight,
With crickets doing jazz and a firefly light.
I join the fiesta, with two left feet,
As the shadows of palms sway to the beat.

A squirrel spins tales of his acorn stash,
While I spill my drink in a not-so-cool splash.
But laughter abounds, as my friends gather near,
With branches a'wiggling, they cheer and they cheer.

So here's to the mischief that nature can brew,
With giggles and wiggles and moments anew.
Nestled dreams swirl, in this riotous scene,
Where leaves whisper secrets only we have seen.

Secrets of the Verdant Realm

In this secret garden, where whimsy takes flight,
A rabbit takes charge—he's our comic knight.
With hopscotch adventures, he leads us along,
While chattering birds join in our song.

The groundhogs are plotting a cheeky surprise,
While I try to keep up, oh what a rise!
The ferns wave hello, with a tickle and tease,
As I dodge a low branch, quite pleased with the breeze.

Amidst all the giggling and raucous delight,
A lizard does yoga, what a curious sight!
The palms clap in rhythm, as shadows parade,
As laughter escapes in this verdant charade.

As evening descends with a blanket of stars,
Our escapades echo like stories from Mars.
With secrets aplenty beneath leafy walls,
Forever entwined in nature's great calls.

Poetry of the Whispering Wind

The breeze tells jokes to the leaves,
They giggle and wiggle, swaying with ease.
A squirrel eavesdrops, snickers and darts,
Imagining acorns as comedic arts.

The sun peeks through with a cheeky grin,
While shadows dance like siblings in sin.
A bird thinks it's a star on the vine,
Singing its heart out, feeling divine.

A lizard suns with a fashionable pose,
While ants march in line, donning their clothes.
Nature's a circus, a playful parade,
Where laughter's the ticket, none need to pay.

Even the flowers join in the fun,
With colors so bright, they outshine the sun.
At dusk, fireflies waltz, oh what a sight!
Under this canopy, all feels just right.

Glimmers of Serenity Among the Trees

Beneath the branches, a picnic unfolds,
Squirrels drop snacks, or so I've been told.
Amidst the laughter, the roots intertwine,
Like old friends who share every last wine.

The seats are made soft by nature's own quilt,
With toppings of moss and a hint of silk.
Crickets recite the best of their tunes,
As frogs croak along under bright silver moons.

A sunbeam takes aim at a hide-and-seek,
Sunkissed disguise, giggling's not bleak.
Posing like models, the trees sway with flair,
The whole scene's a riot—join in if you dare!

A breeze spins round, causing hats to fly,
While picnickers chase them without any shy.
Amidst the fun in this leafy grand stage,
Life writes its humor on nature's own page.

Moments Captured in Nature's Embrace

In a corner of green, where laughter bestows,
A rabbit prances, wearing bright bows.
While daisies gossip, the sun starts to fade,
Decreeing that playtime's a joyful charade.

A turtle jogs slow with comedic flair,
While tiny bugs play tag in the air.
Nearby a chameleon looks for a snack,
But ends up camouflaged—what a move, what a hack!

Puppies chase shadows, in the golden light,
And tumble around, what a comical sight!
While owls look on with wisdom so deep,
They chuckle at antics, while still half-asleep.

Every moment's captured in nature's own frame,
With jesters and jest, it's all part of the game.
As stars begin twinkling, the night starts to hum,
In this playful embrace, we're all feeling fun.

Dappled Dreams Beneath the Fronds

Under draping leaves, there's a whimsical air,
Where frogs wear tuxedos, tassels and flair.
The sun plays tricks, casting spots on the ground,
While nature's own cartoons dance round and round.

A breeze whispers tales of the mischief it's seen,
While squirrels concoct pranks with a festive cuisine.
A grin spreads wide, as they scurry along,
The forest leads with a merry old song.

With dappled light twirling, the scene comes alive,
Where butterflies giggle and bees take a dive.
A flower winks, though it knows it's a tease,
As caterpillars plot just to bring it to knees.

As dusk softly settles, the fun doesn't cease,
Fireflies join in, offering lightness and peace.
Beneath all those fronds, laughter lingers and streams,
In this dappled world, we all chase our dreams.

Embraced by the Island Breeze

A crab in shades, feeling quite cool,
He dances along like a cheerful fool.
The coconut falls, a thud on the sand,
While seagulls giggle, thinking it's grand.

The sun wears a hat, so bright and bold,
And folks on the shore are too hot to hold.
A kid builds a castle, forgets where he stands,
As waves play tag with his tiny plans.

An iguana struts, with swagger and flair,
While tourists start snapping — what a bizarre affair!
A beach ball bounces into a piña colada,
A splash and a laugh, oh what a bravada.

The evening brings laughter, a bonfire's glow,
As friends swap their tales of summer's flow.
They dance in the night, under stars that tease,
Embraced by the warmth of the island breeze.

Twilight Tales of the Tropics

In twilight's glow, a parrot does squawk,
Telling shy secrets while on a rock.
A fisherman winks, his net full of fish,
His catch dances too, oh what a dish!

The hammock sways in a gentle swoon,
As crickets join in, a tropical tune.
A turtle named Bob has lost track of the time,
He yawns in the sun, dreaming of lime.

Drinks in hand, stories flow like a stream,
Friends laugh over antics that seemed like a dream.
A pig in a lei joins the evening parade,
While the moon rolls her eyes at the antics displayed.

As night paints the sky in swirls of delight,
Laughter erupts, chasing away the fright.
In this place where the stories intertwine,
Twilight tales sparkle with humor divine.

Whispers Beneath the Fronds

Under leafy palms where the shadows play,
A monkey swings by, has something to say.
With cheeky little grins, he tosses a fruit,
Oh, what a show, this silly pursuit!

A lizard in sunglasses, basking with glee,
Coordinates sunbathing with utmost decree.
While tourists fumble with all their gear,
The sun hums a tune that tickles the ear.

The breeze carries laughter from kids on the shore,
A splash in the water, then laughter galore.
A crab attempts dance, and oh, what a sight!
The rhythm of nature, pure comedic delight.

As dusk settles in, with stars looking bright,
They gather 'round fire, sharing laughs of the night.
With whispers of joy and chuckles unplanned,
Life's silly moments, hand in hand.

Beneath the Canopy's Embrace

Beneath the green arch, a squirrel holds court,
With acorns and stories, he's never cut short.
He flicks his tail, in a fashion so grand,
While the world stops to listen, a tiny bandstand.

A funny parade of flip-flops and shorts,
As beach bums lounge with amusing retorts.
Each sip of cold drink brings giggles anew,
With sand in their hair, sipping lost in the blue.

The moon's shining brightly, a glowing big smile,
As crabs hold a meeting, all in a file.
They talk of great journeys, of tides and of shuns,
In their crusty old way, cracking jokes 'bout the runs.

The night rounds off with a whimsical cheer,
With friendships ignited, and nothing to fear.
In this haven of laughter, with humorous grace,
What joy it is, beneath this warm embrace.

Beneath the Tropical Veil

Under the leaves, I once did hide,
A squirrel claimed my snack with pride.
Coconuts fell, what a loud clatter,
I laughed so hard, my sides did splatter.

The sunbeams dance, a jolly sight,
A parrot squawks without a fright.
I tried to mimic, but fell from grace,
He flew away, left me with my face.

A hammock swings in breezy air,
I nod off quick without a care.
The lizards laugh as I snooze away,
Dreaming of snacks, both night and day.

The breeze brings tales, oh what a tease,
Of coconut crabs who wear blue jeans.
They scuttle by, a sight so rare,
Do they have parties? I must prepare!

The Solace of Swaying Shadows

Dancing leaves make a playful sound,
While the sun plays hide and seek around.
A tortoise spies, with crafty glee,
Making a race, bet you can't see!

Bananas peel like jokes untold,
As monkeys swing, getting bold.
With every leap, they steal a bite,
Leaving me giggling at their flight.

Under the palms, I forge a seat,
Ants march by in a comic feat.
They turn and salute, oh what a fuss,
Just a friendly band on their way to discuss!

As night falls in, the crickets sing,
Telling tales of mishaps they bring.
I join along, with a wink and a cheer,
Among the shadows, I have no fear!

Sunlight Through the Lattice

Sunlight weaves through green and gold,
Twirling shadows, never old.
A lizard peeks with a cheeky grin,
While I sip my drink, feeling the spin.

Frogs croak loud, casting silly bets,
On who can leap the highest—no regrets.
I chant along, "Go slimy green!"
What a spectacle, a lively scene!

Wind-blown laughter, a feathery song,
The breeze hums sweet, can't go wrong.
A toucan poses, a true diva,
While I awkwardly dance, looking like a piece of pizza.

The lattice shadows make me sway,
As I dance like nobody's watching, hey!
With every misstep, I shake and shout,
"Join the fun, doubt's out!"

Secrets of the Silent Grove

In this grove, whispers float so free,
The palm fronds gossip, just you and me.
I croak like a frog, it's my hidden skill,
Pretty sure the trees find it a thrill.

A sneaky gecko, oh what a sport,
He tries to blend in, guess it's his forte.
I cheer him on, the champion of stealth,
While pineapples giggle, oh what good health!

When the coconut falls, I leap in fright,
Imagining it's a meteorite!
With a bounce and a roll, I watch it descend,
Did I just become dinner? Not this weekend!

The night brings stars, a glowing show,
We dance like nobody will ever know.
Beneath the whispered tales we weave,
In this silent grove, I truly believe!

Wanderlust Under the Green Canopy

Under canopies, I often roam,
Chasing lizards far from home.
A tiny bird, it steals my hat,
I chase it down, oh fun is that!

Swinging vines, a jungle gym,
Trying not to trip and swim.
With every twist, I tumble down,
And laugh like a silly clown.

Sipping coconuts with a straw,
While dodging bites of gnarly jaw.
Monkeys giggle, throwing beans,
Life here feels like in-between dreams.

I find a bench to catch my breath,
A place to ponder life and death.
But then the ants have other plans,
They march, they march, in tiny bands.

Glimmers of Hope in the Shade

I peek beneath the leafy veil,
A squirrel spins a funny tale.
With acorns flying every day,
I laugh, I dodge, hip-hip-hooray!

The sun laughs too, in patches bright,
As shadows dance and spark delight.
I try to skip from tree to tree,
But roots trip me, oh look at me!

A toad croaks out his croaky song,
While butterflies dance along.
I clap my hands and start to twirl,
To join the fun of this wild world.

Hope glimmers like the dappled rays,
In this green realm where laughter stays.
I take a leap, embrace the cheer,
With every chuckle, I feel them near.

Rhythms of the Tropical Night

As night unfolds, the crickets chirp,
They pull me in, my thoughts they stir.
With fireflies lighting up the air,
I sway and spin without a care.

Bananas dangle like disco balls,
Each twist and turn, my awkward falls.
The moon takes charge, and soon I groan,
A friendly breeze decides to play clone.

Rats and raccoons join my dance,
With mischievous grins, they take a chance.
Laughter bubbles, the rhythms sway,
In this tropical night, I find my way.

A conga line of mixed-up mates,
We shake and giggle, such silly states.
Under stars that wink and shine,
Life spins by, and it feels divine.

A Journey Through Leafy Labyrinths

I wander through this leafy maze,
With twists and turns to set ablaze.
A garden path, a mystery,
With whispers hiding history.

Oh, what's that rustle in the leaves?
A snake? A frog? Oh, how it weaves!
With every step, I make some noise,
And mirth erupts, oh joyful joys.

The ferns are soft, a pillow quick,
I plop right down and take a pick.
What's the best snack here in this zone?
Oh, wait—a beetle? Just my own!

I chart my course with giggles bright,
Each leafy turn, a pure delight.
In this green realm, I lose my way,
Yet find my heart where laughter stays.

Rituals of Sun and Shade

Birds in the trees like gossiping friends,
Chirping about where the daylight ends.
Squirrels in suits, holding grand debates,
On the best acorns and pilfered plates.

Laying on grass, with a hat on my face,
Wondering if shade is a magical place.
The sun plays tricks, a game of hide-and-seek,
While skaters slip by, looking quite chic.

Drinks with umbrellas in bright hues parade,
I toast to the fronds, my sunburn's upgrade.
Shady alliances, we laugh and we cheer,
As the world spins slowly, let's all drink beer!

Beneath the great trees, life dances and sways,
In the warmth of the sun, we plan our next phase.
A picnic of nonsense, a feast for the fleet,
We gather our laughter, a summertime treat.

Beneath the Gaze of Watchful Fronds

Frogs leap in sync, a comedic ballet,
Each jump a performance, come join the fray!
Lizards on logs, sunbathing too,
Rolling their eyes, in colorful view.

Bees buzz with gusto, a busy brigade,
While flowers spin tales of their sweet escapade.
Caterpillars munch, on a leaf buffet,
Laughing at ants, in their suit-and-tie ballet.

Picking a coconut, a game gone awry,
The hard nut refuses, it's high in the sky.
Jokes in the air, like a mirage of fun,
We drop it together; oh look! It's not done!

Amidst the great trunks, we share silly pranks,
Imagining pirates, wearing washed-out planks.
Under the gaze of the fronds all around,
We revel in laughter, our joy truly found.

The Lush Embrace of Serenity

Coconuts drop like little bombs,
Sending us running with giggles and qualms.
The breeze at our backs, tickles our ears,
As palm trees hide our childish jeers.

A picnic mat sprawled, with snacks piled high,
Between fruity dances and the clouds in the sky.
Sandwiches grumble, they're losing their fight,
But we feast on laughter, our greatest delight!

Sun-soaked retreats lead to sandy disputes,
Over who can throw the best funny hoots.
Watermelons fumble, splat on the floor,
As we roll with the laughter, pleading for more!

The breeze keeps us cool, like a humorous tease,
Each moment together, a burst of pure ease.
Here in this haven of mirth and of fun,
We live like the children, forever in sun!

Twilight's Serenade Beneath the Canopy

As dusk settles in, crickets spark a tune,
The palms start to sway, sharing secrets with the moon.
Fireflies twinkle, like stars on the ground,
Creating a dance where giggles abound.

The raccoons are plotting, they're sneakily wise,
With snacks in their paws, oh what a surprise!
They scuttle in shadows, plotting their fate,
While we gather our stories, feeling quite great.

Jokes around campfires, where shadows can laugh,
And the flames crackle tales, an odd epitaph.
Marshmallows toast in a comical fight,
As folks make sweet smiles, by fire's warm light.

Under the stars, with palms standing tall,
We reminisce about nothing and everything at all.
The twilight serenade, a whimsical delight,
In this lush paradise where laughter takes flight.

Beneath the Whispering Canopies

Underneath leafy giants, we play,
Giggles echo, as squirrels relay.
A lime fell, bonked Timmy on head,
Now he's convinced, it's a fruit war ahead!

The lizards lounge like they own the scene,
Winking their eyes, oh so obscene.
Chasing shadows, we trip on the grass,
Imitating their moves, what a silly mass!

A coconut drops with a thud on the ground,
We laugh so hard, we roll all around.
Nature's jesters, we join in the fun,
Juggling fruit till the day is done!

As twilight fades, laughter persists,
The trees share secrets, in nature's twists.
Amidst the echoes, we make a pact,
To never grow up, and that's a fact!

Secrets of the Swaying Fronds

Whispers float by on a playful breeze,
Plants gossip loudly, if only you please.
A palm leaf smirks, with a swing and a wave,
It tells us tales, of the foolish and brave.

In the green depths, mischief unfolds,
Tales of lost sandals and adventures bold.
The crickets chirp, keeping perfect time,
While we hone our skills for the acorn climb!

A banana peel's been left on the path,
Off we tumble, oh what a laugh!
Nature is jesting, with humor so prime,
It's a comedy stage, as we mime in rhymes!

The sky turns pink, as the sun bids adieu,
We're still giggling, don't know what to do.
The fronds, they sway, whispering delight,
Promising mischief 'til the end of night!

Sunlight and Silhouettes

Sunlight bursts through, igniting the day,
Making shadows dance, in the funniest way.
Pretend to be giants, as we stretch very tall,
Yet down we go—oops! Now we're small!

Our silhouettes cast on the ground like a play,
A dragonfly zooms past, or was it a ray?
Imitating birds, we hop on one foot,
Chasing the shadows, in a big cartoon suit!

The sunbeams tickle with their golden embrace,
While we strike poses, making silly face.
Twirling like dancers, emotions they sway,
Basking in laughter, while the bright secures play!

As evening approaches, the silliness fades,
Recollection of antics, our laughter cascades.
Tomorrow we'll come, for a brand new set,
Dancing in sunlight, without any fret!

When Leaves Dance with the Wind

Leaves perform ballet, spinning all around,
As we belly-laugh, at the antics we've found.
A gust whips by, a sweep that we feel,
We chase after breeze, with an endearing squeal!

In the middle of chaos, a picnic takes flight,
Sandwiches soar, oh what a sight!
Chasing crumbs down the grassy hill,
We roll in fits, with a pantry thrill!

The wind's a prankster, tossing trees' tops,
We gather together, for unlikely pops.
With branches that sway, we conspire in jest,
Planning our climb for the very next quest!

Dusk starts to settle, but we still feel bold,
Crickets' soft singing tells tales of old.
As leaves drift away in the twilight's embrace,
We promise, tomorrow, we'll return to this place!

The Scent of a Distant Shore

Seagulls squawk like honking cars,
A crab waves hello from the stars.
Wet sand clings like a clingy friend,
Shells sing tales that never end.

The breeze brings whispers of old fish,
Someone's lunch becomes my wish.
Fried calamari is a delight,
Caught my toe; it gave me a fright.

Coconuts tumble on the ground,
Bouncy like balls, round and profound.
A flip-flop flew, hit a beachy chap,
He laughed so hard, fell in the lap.

The scent of salt fills the air,
Tanned with humor, without a care.
Sun-kissed smiles under summer's sun,
Dancing like crabs; oh what fun!

Hushed Conversations of the Night

The crickets chirp in a secret code,
As fireflies twinkle and light the road.
A cat's meow echoes, distant yet near,
Whispers of laughter float through the clear.

Flip-flops slap like an awkward dance,
While the stars above seem to glance.
Oh, watch out! A raccoon snatches a snack,
Leaving us gasping; he's got no lack!

Moonbeams flicker on the velvet ground,
While shadows play hopscotch, jumping around.
"Who's there?" my friend teases in fright,
"Just the breeze!" I say, "And a ghostly bite!"

The night giggles as the crickets play,
A symphony of odd in bright array.
In the dark, we chuckle, we jest,
With nature's quirks, we are truly blessed.

Beneath the Leaves' Embrace

The branches wave like an old-time show,
While ants march by in a line, so slow.
A twig snaps, sending squirrels in flight,
They skitter and scatter, what a sight!

Beneath the leaves, a sunbeam peeks,
Tickling my nose; oh, nature speaks!
"Don't take that nap!" the lizard scolds,
"Get up, get moving, the day unfolds!"

A lazy breeze tells jokes to the flowers,
They giggle softly for hours and hours.
Just then, my hat sails away with glee,
It dances, it twirls, a runaway spree!

The foliage whispers secrets quite grand,
All around us, nature takes a stand.
With laughter and light, we roam and play,
Under leafy arms where fun finds a way.

Resonance of the Rustling Palms

Palms sway like dancers, all in a row,
Trading tall tales with a breezy flow.
A parrot squawks riddles in the air,
While toucans giggle, without a care.

The rustle speaks in a leafy tone,
Tickling our ears, like a funny phone.
A coconut drops; we all duck low,
"Head's up!" we yell, but it's filled with dough?

Lizards dart past, chasing their tails,
While ants enact tiny train trails.
"Watch out, it's coming!" a friend shouts in glee,
A stray beach ball bounces, and oh, how we flee!

In the palm's embrace, our laughter ignites,
With nature's chorus on tropical nights.
Each rustle a giggle, a cheeky grin,
Life's a wild ride; let the fun begin!

The Color of Shadows and Light

A squirrel slipped on a big green leaf,
Caught in a dance, no time for grief.
The sun peeked through with a cheeky grin,
While shadows played hide and seek with him.

Lizards trying out their sliding tricks,
On sun-kissed rocks, in a mix of kicks.
With laughter from birds, they join the cheer,
While a cat watches closely, with plans unclear.

Breezes whispered gossip, oh so sly,
Tickling the grass, making it fly.
A bug in a hurry, what's his grand scheme?
He tripped on a shadow, lost in a dream.

With colors so vibrant, a jester parade,
Life under canopies, where antics are made.
Laughter, oh laughter, as day turns to night,
In the play of the shadows, pure delight!

Tales Told by the Silent Fronds

Fronds gossip softly in the warm air,
Sharing their tales, like a playful dare.
A breeze carries whispers, light as a feather,
Old fables of fruit, and much, much better.

The ants marching proudly on their long quest,
In rows they parade, never taking a rest.
A spider waves high from her silken domain,
While beetles complain, 'Oh, what a pain!'

A raccoon with style, in sunglasses bright,
Danced through the shadows, what a sight!
While chattering monkeys cast silly spells,
Underneath the fronds, where laughter dwells.

One tree, so tall, watched it all from above,
And giggled at drama, just like a glove.
As twilight descended, creatures took flight,
In the emerald realm, oh what a night!

Cradle of Life in the Shade

Under the boughs, where the cool winds play,
A picnic unfolds in a bright ballet.
Baskets spill snacks, a feast on the ground,
With crumbs for the birds, oh joyous sound!

A dog with a hat, goofy as can be,
Chases his tail like a whirlpool spree.
Children laugh loudly, their voices a song,
While ants are planning where they belong.

Old folks swap stories with a smile so wide,
Sharing old jokes, those they once tried.
With eyes twinkling bright, they remember the fun,
As shadows grow longer, the day's almost done.

And as evening falls, with a wink and a sigh,
Stars will appear in the velvet sky.
The shade holds them close, where laughter won't fade,
In a cradle of life, joyfully laid.

The Dusk's Embrace of Green Giants

As dusk tiptoes in, green giants stand tall,
Casting long shadows that tickle and sprawl.
With a wink from the moon, and mischief in tow,
The jesters of nature put on quite a show.

The crickets compose a symphony grand,
While frogs suit up for a night-time band.
Each note is a giggle, each chirp a cheer,
Under the cover, where all's crystal clear.

Fireflies flicker, like stars gone astray,
Dancing through gardens, in a sprightly ballet.
Revving the shadows, all creatures take flight,
In the embrace of dusk, a magical night.

A wise old owl hoots, "Let the fun commence!"
As shadows collide in a dance of suspense.
With laughter and joy, the forest's alive,
In the twilight's glow, oh, how they thrive!

Reverie in the Grove

Beneath the lofty trees, I tripped,
With roots like snakes, my feet were gripped.
I laughed so loud, the birds took flight,
They left their seeds, to my delight.

A squirrel winked with nutty pride,
Planning a stash he'd smartly hide.
I danced with shadows, shades of glee,
In cubby holes, what sights to see!

The breeze whispered secrets, funny and bold,
Of acorns falling and tales retold.
I grabbed my hat, a mighty palm,
And dreamed of skies, oh, so calm!

Oh, nature's jest, how sweet the jest,
In this green world, I feel so blessed.
With tangled roots and playful sights,
Each moment here, pure delight ignites.

Whispering Dreams Amongst the Leaves

Underneath the leafy guise,
I caught a glimpse of bright blue skies.
A bug in shades, tried to dance,
I giggled hard, what a chance!

The flowers chuckled in the breeze,
Telling jokes with such great ease.
A bumblebee buzzed a silly tune,
As I swayed and hummed along to noon.

I spotted a frog with a crown so grand,
He leaped around like he owned the land.
Sipping dew like morning wine,
He croaked, 'This grove is simply divine!'

So here I laugh with nature's crew,
A raucous scene with laughter true.
Among the leaves where dreams twist and twirl,
Life is a joke, oh what a whirl!

Canopy Tales at Dusk

At dusk, the canopy comes alive,
With stories and tales that thrive.
A lizard in shades, with a dapper flair,
Quipped a wisecrack, without a care.

The twilight chuckled, painted gold,
As crickets chirped, so bold, so old.
I told the stars, 'You shine too bright!'
They winked back, 'We love the night!'

A monkey swung by, with a sly grin,
He stole my hat, oh, where to begin?
We laughed and played, a wild spree,
In this dusk dance, just him and me.

So with the breeze, I shared my cheer,
In tales of joy, with friends so dear.
As dusk wrapped us in playful gleams,
Life turned to laughter, in funny dreams.

Reflections in the Silence of Green

In the quiet green, there's much to find,
A snail rolled by, so slow, so blind.
He winked and said, 'I take my time,'
For laughs, he claimed, are simply prime!

A shadow crept with a secret smile,
As flowers snoozed in their own style.
I joined the hush, tried not to peek,
But bursts of chuckles made me weak.

The rustling leaves began to jest,
Whispering laughs, what a funky fest.
The sun said, 'Lighten up, just play!'
And so I did, in my own way.

So here I dwell, in green so bright,
With nature's charm in laughing light.
In silence sweet, the humor beams,
In every rustle, life's funny dreams.

Lush Life in the Tropic's Grasp

Beneath the leaves so wide and grand,
A squirrel sneaks a coconut in his hand.
He nods to birds with feathers bright,
As they gossip about the moon at night.

The monkeys munch on fruit with grace,
While waving to the odd, lost face.
A toucan laughs, what a sight to see,
As he hangs out with a lazy bee.

A parrot steals a snack from me,
Winks with charm from the tallest tree.
I laugh and chase this feathery thief,
In this green chaos, I find relief.

With sunshine pouring, laughter blends,
In places where the silliness never ends.
Life's just fun in this wild expanse,
Join the chorus—give joy a chance!

Secret Gardens Beneath the Tropics

Whispers echo in the tale of trees,
Where geckos dance and giggle with ease.
Each flower blooms in flamboyant hue,
As cold lemonade waits—oh, what a view!

A rabbit hops with a mischievous grin,
While critters gather for a quirky spin.
They swap their stories and share their treats,
In this lush hideaway where joy repeats.

The sun dips low with a painter's brush,
Crickets come out, oh what a rush!
Belly laughs echo all through the night,
In a garden of wonders, everything's right.

With secret jokes and a playful theme,
Life's a colorful and vibrant dream.
So here I'll stay, under leafy arches,
In this comedy where laughter marches!

In the Embrace of the Whispering Green

In emerald arms, the world feels light,
As frogs serenade with their croaking delight.
Lizards play hide and seek with the breeze,
While friends debate over earthy cheese.

The sun winks down, a playful tease,
Tickling toes of swaying trees.
A parade of ants in a tiny line,
Marching to the tune of a bumblebee's whine.

I spy a sloth with a smile so wide,
Reclining on branches, what a joyful ride!
His lazy giggles keep time with the waves,
In this green embrace, each moment saves.

So grab a chair, pour a drink so cold,
Join the fun, let wild tales unfold.
In the arms of this vibrant scene,
Life's a joke, and we're living the dream!

Solace Found Among Swaying Leaves

A dance of shadows, a flickering play,
As breezes swirl in a gleeful sway.
The foliage chuckles, a rustling cheer,
It cradles my worries, brings laughter near.

A frog in a hat croons a merry tune,
While bees buzz around like tiny balloons.
I join the circus of critters divine,
In this leafy haven, oh how we shine!

The sun starts to fade, but spirits stay high,
As crickets chirp under twilight sky.
Every leaf whispers a secret or two,
In this haven of fun, I'm forever anew.

With nature's jokes and giggles galore,
In the embrace of growth, who could ask for more?
So here I dwell, in laughter's sweet reprieve,
Among swaying leaves, I choose to believe!

The Calm of Green Retreats

Leaves dance with whispers, oh what a show,
A lizard struts by with a confident glow.
Sipping a drink with a silly little straw,
While a squirrel drops nuts, what a comical flaw!

Sunbeams tickle my nose, I let out a sneeze,
Ants march in lines like they own the trees.
A butterfly flutters, thinking it's grand,
While I trip on a root—who knew they could stand?

The breeze plays a tune, it's catchy and light,
As a parrot mimics my laugh, what a sight!
Chasing shadows—oh look, a giant banana,
In this green retreat, who needs a tropicana?

Palm leaves sway gently, they seem to conspire,
To pull off a prank, like a scene on the wire.
Giggles erupt from the grass at my feet,
As the whole jungle joins in on the beat!

Serenade of the Swaying Trees

A squirrel's on stage, performing a feat,
Dancing on branches, it's quite hard to beat.
The trees sway along, giving leafy applause,
While I giggle softly, forgetting my flaws.

Sunshine slips past, painting stripes on the ground,
An old tortoise waddles, moving slow but profound.
A breeze fluffs my hair, like I'm on a show,
As a critter jogs by, with a rather fast flow.

The flowers are laughing, in colors so bold,
Their petals a chorus, in antics untold.
I join in the fun, swinging wildly with glee,
As bees buzz around with their own symphony.

Laughter is echoing through the bright green maze,
As I trip on a root and embrace the sun's rays.
The trees just chuckle, swaying with flair,
In this quirky ballet, I'm light as the air!

Underneath Nature's Embrace

A hammock hangs low with a twist and a flip,
I attempt to climb in, but it's quite a trip.
Ducks gather round, they quack out their tunes,
While I laugh at the antics of tiny raccoons.

The flowers throw shade, all sassy and bright,
A breeze picks up gossip—they're having a night.
Bugs buzz in circles, a tiny parade,
While I swat them away, feeling awkwardly frayed.

The sunlight breaks through, painting spots on my nose,
A curious monkey arrives with a pose.
He steals my snack, then he flashes a grin,
In this nature's embrace, I can't help but win!

As shadows stretch longer, the laughter does bloom,
The trees sway in rhythm, it feels like a room.
I snicker and wiggle, oh what a delight,
In this whimsical dance, nature's love shines bright!

Shadows in a Tropical Hideaway

Under leafy canopies, where giggles collide,
I stumble through laughter, nowhere to hide.
A toucan appears, looking oddly bemused,
As I chase my own shadow, quite utterly confused.

The palms huddle close like a band with a plan,
While iguanas sit back, like the world's biggest fan.
I twist and I tango, but trip on a stone,
The lizards just snicker—oh, leave me alone!

Sunset paints pictures in colors so wild,
As I try to keep up—not acting like a child.
With a wink and a wiggle, the fireflies begin,
Their twinkling messengers bringing joy from within.

The night is a canvas, where laughter takes flight,
As the stars join the fun, twinkling bright in the night.
In this tropical hideaway, where chaos prevails,
The creatures and I share our wonky tales!

Instants Caught in the Green Lattice

A squirrel in a hurry, steals my sandwich fast,
While I'm lost in laughter, my picnic's not meant to last.
The ants host a parade, marching in a line,
Uninvited guests at my party, oh isn't that divine?

A bird chortles loudly, with a comedic flair,
It mimics my sneezes, which earns it a glare.
And as I sip my drink, it dives for my fries,
Nature's jugglers and jesters, oh what a surprise!

The sun shines with mischief, peeking through the trees,
Tickling my nose gently, teasing with a breeze.
I'm wrestling with my hat, as it takes to the air,
A battle of wits with a gust, it's not really fair.

Giggling at the stories, that the shadows tell,
Every twist and turn seems like a jester's spell.
So, I join the chaos, let the fun never cease,
Under this green lattice, I find my little peace.

Reverie Under the Leafy Canopy

A cat naps above me, sprawled out on a limb,
While beneath, I ponder, is life a playful whim?
A frog starts to croak, thinking it's a star,
With every ribbit, I'm scoping out the bizarre.

The breeze plays a tune, rustling all the leaves,
Making up verses that no one believes.
I chuckle at the notion, that dreams take their flight,
In this leafy haven, everything feels just right.

Squirrels scuttle laughing, chasing their own tails,
While butterflies are gossiping, exchanging their tales.
A shadowed giggle erupts from a passing bee,
Thinking it's the comedian, buzzing joyfully.

This realm of delight, where antics abound,
Every nook holds a laugh, every shadow a sound.
Nestled in lightheartedness, moments drift by,
Underneath the leafy roof, where laughter can fly.

Hidden Stories of the Sweltering Shade

In the cozy coolness, where whispers are spun,
A raccoon scouts for snacks, thinking it's so fun.
He fancies himself sneaky, wearing his disguise,
Yet, his antics unfold, under watchful eyes.

With a mischievous grin, the sun starts to peek,
As if joining in on the playful critique.
A turtle stretches slowly, claiming a prime spot,
While I laugh at the chaos, forgetting my thoughts.

Crickets hold a concert, chirping in tune,
As butterflies flitter past, like color butoon.
Each moment's a giggle, wrapped snug in the shade,
Where hidden stories thrive, in this funny charade.

Time ticks in a jest, as shadows play games,
Under this sweltering throne, nothing stays the same.
Here in this calm chaos, life teaches with glee,
That each laugh shared in secret, is a gift to be free.

The Silent Chorus of Swaying Trees

Whispers ride the wind, secrets held so tight,
As branches sway with laughter, tickling morning light.
A wobbly woodpecker, plays a drum solo there,
While squirrels join the chorus, in this woodland fair.

The shadows dance in circles, causing quite a scene,
As rabbits leap like actors, in their leafy green.
Each movement a punchline, nature's own delight,
Echoing through the laughter, of a joyous light.

Nearby a lizard struts, with an air of finesse,
While all around him linger, the crickets cackle, no less.
Their rhythm matches well, to the leaves' soft sway,
And here beneath the trees, we all join in the play.

So here in silent splendor, fun blooms everywhere,
As I breathe in the laughter feels lighter than air.
Wrapped up in this moment, where joy truly thrives,
The silent chorus sings, and it feels like we're alive.

www.ingramcontent.com/pod-product-compliance
Lightning Source LLC
Chambersburg PA
CBHW072217070526
44585CB00015B/1373